Cantata in Two Voices

Cantata in Two Voices

Jude Neale & Bonnie Nish

Ekstasis Editions

Published in 2018 by:
Ekstasis Editions Canada Ltd.
Box 8474, Main Postal Outlet
Victoria, B.C. V8W 3S1

Ekstasis Editions
Box 571
Banff, Alberta T1L 1E3

LIBRARY AND ARCHIVES CANADA CATALOGUING IN PUBLICATION

Neale, Jude, author
    Cantata in two voices / Jude Neale and Bonnie Nish.

Poems.
Issued in print and electronic formats.
ISBN 978-1-77171-279-8 (softcover).--ISBN 978-1-77171-280-4 (ebook)

    I. Nish, Bonnie, author II. Title.

PS8627.E22C36 2018   C811'.6   C2018-901318-4
                                                 C2018-901319-2

Canada Council   Conseil des Arts   Funded by the   Canada
for the Arts   du Canada   Government
                                            of Canada

Ekstasis Editions acknowledges financial support for the publication of *Cantata in Two Voices* from the government of Canada through the Canada Book Fund and the Canada Council for the Arts, and from the Province of British Columbia through the Book Publishing Tax Credit.

Printed and bound in Canada.

To Katie and Jer
Sebastian, Becca and Ali

Poetry is just the evidence of life.
If your life is burning well, poetry is
just the ash.

Leonard Cohen

Contents

Foreword

It has been a delight and challenge to weave our two poetic voices into a single book of poems. We took turns choosing the epigraph and all subsequent responses to this trigger. We met in person only once and conceived and created each poem on the internet with one writer taking on the job of editor. We felt we needed to have a consistent eye to allow both voices to be heard in a unified form. As the work unfolded our words began a dance that quickly turned closely around one another, unique but usually in sync – the final edits caught the spaces where we stepped too far away.

Because of the nature of the project we collaborated on all aspects of the writing. We set a goal to write a book in fifty days allowing for the fifty pages to complete our manuscript. After intense and exhilarating exchange of ideas we are proud to introduce our work, *Cantata in Two Voices*.

We hope you enjoy reading the dozens of epigraphs by an international pantheon of poets. We both felt these were the key to inspiration and acted like an unwrapped gift, just waiting to be discovered.

This is a completely unique collection of poems, written by two experienced poets and based on the words of other writers.

We hope you are transformed in some small way by Cantata in Two Voices.

Jude Neale/Bonnie Nish

The Word

There is no happiness like mine.
I have been eating poetry.
Ink runs from the corners of my mouth.
   Mark Strand, "Eating Poetry"

I string words like pearls
across the verdant landscape
of my mind.

They walk with me,
every mile held together

with meaning so clear,
that the nouns and verbs
paint a pointillist painting.

My fingers are slick with rhyme,
as I am thrown back
into a dizzying reverie
of mood and distance.

I catch them like starfish
and press each of them firmly
onto my fresh page,

where they stand together,
sway with context or whimsy.

I write a poem juicy
as a wet pomegranate,
dripping down hot flesh.

Or find one hiding shyly
In the dusty recesses
of stubborn memory.

All of this I know today,

when all I asked for
was just one good line –

stuck together
with the paste of good living
and the hardships slow grind.

Only You

When the wind turns and asks, in my father's voice,
Have you prayed?
    Li-Young Lee, "Have You Prayed?"

I have answered too many questions
as the wind blows through the house.

I have bent low on my knees,
an origami body folded in with suffering.

The words of the dead imprint on my tongue.

I have flown from knowing your tears,
a river of silver, a river of blood,

to wearing your heart
on my sleeve.

I call your name beautiful,
though it dissolves like smoke
behind a mirror of tears.

I have a chalice
for this filigreed grief,
as the dust of a 1000 dead lilies
leaves a bridge

only you can cross.

What Is Not Mine

Inside the box, two flaking albums their pages loose.
  John Steffler

How can I see you when the dark
is in the way of your perfection?

Your old hand
can't even
fold tissue
into squares

where secrets float.

Now, no one else cares
about these black and white photos.
Dust covers of memory
slipped between our fingers.

I can't capture the silence,
the unsung melody,
of the Blue Danube Waltz.

The dances of your youth
that whirled you
into the bright orange sky,

where black-lined stockings
and Jimmy Dean hair
found you wishing for more.

Your cigarette stuck behind your ear,
and your tee-shirt rolled
just above your biceps.

A rebellion in dress walking my way.

You tried to hold me
in your hooded eyes,
but I put you down

afraid,

to take what is not mine.

Angels

The thing about living in a Big City is that you so easily disappear
    Bonnie Nish, "The Big City"

He has become a fish bowl
turned over on its side.

Glass and steel
leave him hostage.

He struggles to be above water again,
his nostrils expand into gills.

He protests the act of being still,
of not being still.
The police cars, the lights,
the smell of piss, are his home.

He lives on exhaust fumes.

Falls into a bed of concrete,
never expecting a soft hand
to hold him.

He's surprised by the kindness of strangers,

swallows it haltingly
into the hollow of his belly
and grows tired from stale gratitude.

Water

After the light coloured shallows the deep river is our resting place
    Kwame Dawes

We don't stand here alone.
We have come from water
to join our torn pasts.

Sea anemone and tall grass
break our in-held breath.

Escaping
into wilderness I rise
like the wind on seafoam.

I want to return to a time
when death didn't stalk us.
When the whisper
of the reeds was enough.

We stood back to back
protecting the shore
from the storm. It arched
round the rocks.

I remembered
lightning and shadows
holding us close in the rain.

We became part
of ocean and pond,

in the muddy torrents running
over the boulders and stones.

Rebirth

In the mountains, stillness;
    Robert Haas, "After Goethe"

I come to this place to find
the depth of wonderment
I have lost in ordinary life.

The pine scented earth
gives up its light
and my bruises fall away.

I am once again whole.

My toes inhale the raspy air
and I move like a mountain spring
coming back to its source.

Now I can open and bloom
and spread out into the dusk,

where Lupines and Indian Paintbrush
carpet the scree.

Slashes of purple-throated
Fireweed snatches at my breath.

Night begins to fall
and everything silent
holds me.

Come to Me

You came to me
Before you know what kindness really
is you must lose things
    Naomi Shihab Nye, "Before you know what kindness really is"

When my father died,
I was the closed drawstring of a silk purse,
you came to me, offered your hand.
When I couldn't see my way out
of the labyrinth I was lost in,
you came to me, offered your eyes.
When the way I had known to be in the world
disappeared and threw me off balance,
you came to me, offered your smile.
When the bitter taste of tears
pulled at my heart,
you came to me, offered your light.
When I lost my footing
trying to find the rising moon,
you came to me, offered your dance.
When the storms brewed inside me
and caused me to duck and hide,
you came to me, offered your shelter.
When I lay down at night to the hum
of your sweet breath,
you came to me,
offered your arms.

La Belle qui fut heaulmière

She gave up beauty
in her tender youth
    Christine Rossetti, "The Portrait"

I used to believe in the things
that only hands could touch.

When the mirror of age
cracked my reflection

I had to search below
the shattered pieces

to find what I was looking for.

The smile of the girl
half-hidden there,

a ghost, a celebration, a plea.

A remembrance of a time
when limbs moved like wind.

My hair blew across my eyes,

in the car when auntie
called me *handsome*,

and I cried for the truth.

I wanted to disappear,
be carried away. To feel

the dross of my body
dissolve beneath me,

never again betrayed.

Well of Sorrow, Well of Light

At the end of my suffering
there was a door.
    Louise Gluck, "The Wild Iris"

Light from a thousand unseen suns
waits just behind my eyes.

I shine a flare for weary travelers.

The snap of the wind
and the magenta tulips
brought me back home,

far away from
the bleak December
woman I had become.

Relief in the knowing
I didn't need to carry

the burden
of everyone's griefs.

I cradle this day in my hands,
careful not to spill

the phosphorescent moments,
waiting for me on the other side.

More Than I Can Hold

Mango drops its fit into my hand
Bends me gently at the wrist with its wet weight
    Lori Cayer, "Mango, Without You"

My lips drew up
around a sliver of ice,

cooling the heat rising
from my belly, groin, thighs.

My torso wrapped in a scream.
Pain pumped like hot coals on feet,

as I pushed
and I cried
to meet you.

You slipped your bonds,

slid like the ark
between my
trembling knees.

I felt your sparrow's breath
graze my wet skin
and met it with joy.

Your language was the sound
of water breaking.

You opened your eyes
into a bright sky,

suckled a fist
clenched so tight,
it squeezed air
into your tiny lungs.

You burst into impatient song,
needing to be heard.

My child,
you weighed more

than my heart
could ever hold.

A Falling Apart

We did not realize it was so near
  Alice Major, "Here"

Dark comes at night,
a death, a falling apart.

I never realized
when you were done.

Couldn't imagine
the walk into cold waters
that crisp morning.

The geese arced and cried
across the sky,

as if they knew about pain
and the keen desire
to rise above it all.

But what drops
from the heavens
pushes us
further to the edge.

You questioned all
that sat in your lap
as truth.

On that cool morning
a quarter of a century later,

the dark still comes at night.

Your death, my falling,
the loss of my best friend.

The cold waters
that swallowed you,

left me chilled to the bone.

Spring Fever

My father was a good crier
and my mother would sink
like meringue
on to the great spears
of skunk cabbage
     Jude Neale, "He'll Be Sorry"

Spring fluttered its embrace
in the early dawn.
I was full and sap happy
In the blossom-smudged air.

These were the crystal
moments left untouched.

I held on to faith in white peonies.
Their innocent faces a confabulation
of ripe and perfumed memory.

Hold me like this
when I lie down beside you.

Know the fragrance of love
for a hundred more years.

Our songs will tell tales
of lemony kisses,

when we became
resplendent with
colour and light.

My Small Sins

We wanted to confess our sins but there were no takers.
White clouds refused to accept them, and the wind
Was too busy visiting sea after sea.
    Czeslaw Milosz, "At A Certain Age"

When I was a child
I wanted to be a Saint.

You said I needed an altar.

So I built it on your back,

for you could hold
the weight of my small sins.

When I was older
I wanted to be a teacher.

You said I needed a glass classroom.

So I burrowed in through your eyes,

For you were the knowledge
I needed to hold.

Then I traded in
my bright purity,
for a chance
to become a priestess of touch.

For you were a prayer shawl
I draped round my neck.

Then I sent everything
I learned into a cloud,
so I could float
into your arms.

For you were the rainstorm
that held all my tears.

Later when I came to you
unfurling my pain,

you said I should kneel
down on broken glass.
For nothing cuts deeper
than this thin slice
of an unspoken dream.

Something to Lean On

The dead in their sheer
open parenthesis, what they
wouldn't give for
something to lean on
that won't give way
    Jorie Graham, "Two Paintings by Gustav Klimt"

She walked on the slack line
sure footed gazelle,

for dust is just dust
and nothing is real.

She twirled with her toes
poised at the moon.

A dangerous dancer
perfectly balanced
on the edge
of this cartegean earth.

Aware the crust
could crack
she leaned
into the wind.

It was the weight of her hunger,
the need to be full
of the daily rave of life
that fueled her core.

Nothing to hang on to,

in this transcendent moment
when the veiled clouds parted,

giving way to the unspeaking night.

Gone but never forgotten

If I could find the world's biggest bags
I would carry them to the end of the road
and dump them into a river of shame.

I would speak of grandfathers,
uncles or teachers, who all took

more than I could ever want to give.
The kiss, the touch, the want buried me,

drove my heart's rhythm
into a tangle of shoe-stringed drum beats,
tripping me every time
I tried to march away.

But I was a compliant niece,
a frightened granddaughter,
a lonely student,

who kept her manners for best –
Sunday dinners and birthday parties.

While in the back rooms
I hid from myself and the road map
being drawn out for the rest of my life,
by cold searching hands.

It had always been mine to give,
the sharp sting of a slap
and a scream pulling my smile
right off of my frozen face.

I tear up this useless guide
drawn out with chalk dust
gathered at my expense,
empty the trash
let the dirt settle.

Now my lips have found a new way
softening the edges of these memories.

That is the woman I have become.

Almost Enough

And another man, who remains inside his own house,
dies there, inside the dishes and in the glasses,
so that his children have to go far out into the
world.
    Rilke, "Somewhere to the east there's a church"

Mary was a woman of earth when she gathered the profusion of fiery snapdragons from her garden to take to the wedding. She sang of true love and glorious endings, to the family and friends of Lloyd, the son of the owner of the general store. They hadn't been further than Kamloops like the rest of the small incestuous village. But Mary the singer and gardener grew dreams of glasses of wine on the banks of the Seine. She let her mind crawl over the rice fields of Cambodia and rested her migrant toes in the clay of the Nile. She held onto facts and figures – knew the stamps of the world in her collection, where she admired the blossoms of Japan or the broad fields of Holland captured in each emblem of a journey, a viewpoint, a change. Then there was the coin collection. She carried the weight of her dreams in the cigar box where she kept them safe. She would one day cash them in when she could afford airfare to the first pinpoint on a map. She hid it in the downstairs cold cellar away from the piercing eyes of her husband, too tired to get anything up, and not old enough to die. Mary sang hymns trembling with hope at funerals. Kept her secrets away from neighbours, who would say *here was enough* and it should be the same for her, and she knew they were wrong.

Towards the light

One might write the history of fire
very briefly: two things rubbing in just the right way
    Jeff Latosik, "The Nuisance of Fire Started by Hand"

When I met you there was fire.

The kind that breathes magic
into a dragon's lair,

or words onto the front page
of a revolution. You were fierce
in your rhetoric, and soft
in your need to touch.

Our arguments
were of Nabokov
and Puccini.

We enflamed
each other's bodies

with whispered fantasies
of the slip and slide
of tongue on skin.

We burnt every shadow
within a hundred-yard radius
just with our eyes,

Each muscle and tendon
ached for you to lay upon me,
stretching your length to mine.

How couldn't you think
of the summer when I wore lilacs
in my hair and you said I was the one?

I could never go back
to being water flowing
uselessly down a deep well.

You set me loose
wild and untamed,
scorching everything
that came between us.
I was a deer leaving my body
running towards the light

infinite beauty of you.

The Gleaming Season

A cool small evening shrunk
to a dog bark and
the clank of a bucket –
And you listening.
    Ted Hughes, "Full Moon and Little Frieda"

In the fall when the crisp leaves
gather round our heads,

we clasp hands, run
at the wind,

as though we could push
the moment to last.

We drop foliage
into a brown paper bag,

for winter when
we need it the most.

We'll clothe it
in Christmas wrap
and green ribbon,

a silent reminder
of those days
when the whip
of a breeze,

picked up my lavender skirt,

and the many hued leaves
nudged wildly at my feet.

It's two in the morning.
The moon hangs low,

a peppermint drop
in the zippered sky.

The moment
between breaths

when I am still and calm,
I'm held here
in the beauty

of the gleaming season,

alone with you
in the thick black night.

Skin Hunger

We lay on a porcelain bed
unbuttoning the night
with our yearning
   Jude Neale, "Unbutton the Night"

My skin is hungry for your touch.

I'm a salmon
swimming upstream.

I battle inertia for a chance
to lean into your sweetness.

You are a freeway
taking me some place
I need to go.

You graze my body with your eyes.

I erupt and try to hold my insides in,
barely breathe, seek out the dance again.

Your hand presses lightly
into the small of my back,
guides me to sparkle and soar,

until I can't stand it anymore,
and circle round your blazing eyes.

I'll break the ring of fire
you dropped at my feet.

This Blank Page

When I thought of daughters
I wasn't expecting this
but I like this more.
    Michael Ondaatje, "To A Sad Daughter"

I married you
at your conception.

I only had room for your taut happiness,
in that chamber of my heart

reserved for canaries and doves.

Every breath
a lilac sprig,
caught
in the bottom
of a drawer.

Know the tender voice of my love.
It will never be broken or bent.

Home will be
in me.

Just as I know with you
I will never be lost,

as your tiny hand sweeps
across mine.

The rhythm of your breath,

the music of our new life,

the first sweet notes inscribed

on this blank page.

Gathered Me In

If they had straightened not veered
    Elise Partridge, "Alternate Histories"

I came from this swamp
never expecting
to be rescued,
by fairy tale frogs.

I was shown the way

by the sunlight on trees,
the spray of white roses,
and the China blue sky.

I ambled along the path,
cuts exposed.

Stranger's hands
washed me clean.

And so life's bruises
evaporated
to aubergine dust.

Here I escaped
on my own,
away from drought
to elixir.

It stoppered
the tears I had saved
during all the lean years.

I became a wolf,
long stride leading me

to splendor on splendor.

The roses, the sea
and the sun,
gathered me in.

City Suite

It could rain all night
with two cats nearby
great shadows making distinct havens
    Mark D. Dunn, "That Famous Wish Deciphered as Lightning"

College Street,
a two-story walk-up
where the sound
of your flute
holds me.

It drowns out the alley cats,
mewling for the morning
meal to come quicker.

I press my ear
to your door,
to capture the song

that slips under the windows,
into the snarl of waiting traffic.

My body curls round your notes,
anticipation building,

for the crescendo and glissando
of your breath.

Again rising for the illusive trill,
trailing to an echo.

The cars below us crawl away,
the cats have fled.

I hear the stone faced
church crack open

with the tolling of bells.

Cicadas

Maybe it is just life's lines
drawn across the palm of
the world
that makes me stay here
        Bonnie Nish, "Until Next Time"

If I listen carefully
I can hear the cicadas
whispering.

I can hear your heart break.

The glass vessel holding
your pain became sealed.

I search for a way to tell you
my love would never leave you,

but I'm mute to your ears.

My words only fly across
a blue-lipped sky,
telling you things
you'd rather forget.

 Cross-legged or fetal position –
 it's all the same.
 Rows of cabbage and poppies
 we carry it all.

The tears and the remembering
grow like weeds in your garden.

I gather them into a bouquet for us to keep.

We will think of this moment,
when we once again hear
the cicadas chirrup and moan.

Waiting

Once confined, he counted the days in sleep
And read the seasons by the way his visitors dressed
    Mark D. Dunn, "He is Still, Moving Through Cages"

You sit alone waiting.

Giraffe-sized lips
form words
that don't make sense.

In the morning when the dogs bark,
you hold your head
in your hands, and pray

someone will stop them
from drilling the hole,
that began at the base
of your skull.

No one stops to say
"How are you Mac?"
"What's going on in there?"

People shoot blank stares
as they fail to see
hope vanishing.

The furrowed night,
has lodged in your memory.

You count the days
by shadow and gloom.

The insidious whine
of the fridge pulls
you deeper down
into the dark.

Time becomes non-linear
as you line up for release,

from this cacophony
that roils round your head.

Is it the belief
that you are sitting
in another world,

singing with Gabriel,

that keeps everyone
listening?

Believe

One night I woke and a white shadow
was trying to get into bed with me.
    Susan Musgrave, "Things That Keep and Do Not Change"

I didn't believe in ghosts
Until the table rose to my waist;
I didn't believe in tables
until I was young and hungry;
I didn't believe in hunger
Until I found no one to love;
I didn't believe in loving
Until I heard you crying;
I didn't believe in tears
Until I slept in a river;
I didn't believe in loneliness
until I felt the absence in my bed;
I didn't believe in distancing
until I saw the fog in your eyes;
I didn't believe in illusions
until the ghosts turned the tables
on my transient disbelief.

Stones From Other's Sorrows

Wide with shadow, his lips fold into his face, his arms are heavy as salt
   Paul Tyler, "The Sad Baker"

He built his house with stones
from other's sorrows,

a reminder of all the shadowed men
who came before him
and fell in mud,

just to be brave.

He was not afraid
of the sweep of sea,
that curled like a tongue
round the sand and shale.

For he had come from red earth,
heavy steps had led him here.

His newspaper memories
rolled into one catastrophic explosion
of morning kisses,
baby's breath and gunfire.

It mixed like tar in his blood.

Even the falling of a leaf
caused him to quake
and yearn,

for the slow drag of time,

when the memories froze
and dreams
were just dreams.

He could still smell
the virulent *Somme*,
mustard gas and bruised sky.

Boys strewn
like wasted petals
onto the ground.

He walked in the still air
holding his pain lightly
behind blinkered eyes.

He can pretend.

Pretend that the air is clear,
and that the children
can be carried and sleep,

without the wrench of his insides

splitting like cedar rail fences,
into the spackled grey sky.

Shimmer

This bright offering
I am unable to take,
This pale one lights up the room.
   Shane Book, "Offering"

Your smile turned heads
whenever you crossed the street.

It did not matter
that your heart lagged behind,

or that your hand's lines
were imprinted with all the lies
you told lovers.

I would not be seduced
by the brightest star again,

for falling is the cost of shining.

You were a strobe light
casting your shimmer like seeds.

And I the lone mirror,
cracked from your gaze.

I fell silent in your shadow,
couldn't see my reflection
when we stood side by side.

Sometimes it's the price of shining
to be shunted aside,
a train off the tracks.

I can't forgive what you have done
for you stole my laughter
with just a glance, and I was repelled
by the smiles I chased.

Look to the dimmer light
to find connection –

the soft brush of the grass,

and the solemn gaze
of the wishing moon
sitting in the silvered trees.

Above It All

The child's cry
Melts in the wall.
And I
Am the arrow,
   Sylvia Plath, "Ariel"

She breathes stars
of air into her lungs,

waiting to explode

into a night
that has no walls.

Expectations drive her
to veer from the straight path,

where she bumps
into edges

and breaks through,
a turtle leaving its shell.

Her black curls press
against the car window.

She watches her mother
come veering
towards her.

Her unholy name
is already formed.

It sails across
the dusty parking lot
and peppers her ears.

She leans into a sky
full of other's stark statements.

Holds onto passing storm clouds
and swallows them,

she ingests their strength.

Lets it sink into her shoes,
buries it in the seams
of her sweater. ·

A wall of thunder protects her
from rage when she's alone –
and she's always alone.

She gathers her need
in blue porcelain cups.

Drinks it down
with the dark
danger of days,

when she's forgotten
how to fly above it all.

Cantata in two voices

I dig up the dirt
> *& tell the rabbi*
to recant
> *his prayer*
I say
> *I do not*
glorify
> *praise*
or bless
> *I do not say*
amen
> Jacob Scheier, "My Mother Dies in Reverse"
> after Robert Priest's *Reading the Bible Backwards*

1.

I cannot walk
> Carrying this load
Without your legs
> I tire and fumble
I fall by the wayside
> Scoop me up
Oh my golden one
> Hold my joys
Dissolve my doubts
> I will rise singing

2.

I cannot speak
     Songs stick in my throat
Without your voice
     I am muted and worn
Caught in a vortex of notes
     Carry me away
With a melody of heart
.   To find love again
The rhythm of our souls
     I will dance once more

3.

In the gloaming of dusk
     The fallen day closes
I watch the sky settle
     Leaves a mantle of light
For we each want more than
     Hearts etched in shadow
One kiss in the moonlight
     When I touch the slow night
Now in this stillness
     I hold slivers of memory
Silken strands bind us
     Like mist to the marsh

From Basket to Treetop

BlackBerry is the colour of a painful bruise on the upper arm, some
internal organ as of yet unnamed.
    Stephanie Bolster, "Many Have Written Poems About Blackberries"

The deep purple of the hydrangea
reflects in the hummingbird's eye.

Slashes of sunlight
streak his ruby head.

I watch transfixed as he flits
from blossom to blossom,

collecting nectar the way
I do dusty memories.

He thrusts the length of his beak
into the throat of the flower.

Drinks the hue of grapes
and the sun spills like syrup

out of the last slice of twilight.

We are the same
always searching

for the sweetness of life,

ignoring the buzzing
of the grey busy city.

But we can't
fly open-mouthed
from basket to treetop,

hauling fragrance and the blur
of summer colour

behind us like a flag.

Truce

In the secular night you wander around
alone in your house. It's two-thirty.
Everyone has deserted you,
or this is your story;
    Margaret Atwood, "In the Secular Night"

Who is here to hold me
If I tremble and fall?

I wander the hospital floor,
catch a whiff of disappointment
mixed with the tang of antiseptic.

The clock on the wall shines
Two-thirty and I want it to end.

Take away the ache that I drag
behind me through the silent ward.

Let my blazing fury ignite
the solace I do not need,

I do not want.

Time is my warden,
the gate keeper
has tricked me into this wild frenzy.

The green gown hugs my thighs.

I slog through another pool
of disappointment I have created.

Polish the white linoed floor
with my torn paper slippers.

I search

for my room with the one thin blanket
draped like a waterfall onto the floor.

I am locked inside,
this ward, this chasm
of emptiness that I must cross.

No one hears but me.
My internal dialogue
swings loosely around
the corners of convictions.

Sentenced to exist within these walls
I sit down resigned.

Hands fold into a bitter prayer,

never quite audible to the nurse
who pats my hand
and says "Sleep."

But I don't sleep. I crawl
towards the dim light
that opens before me,

a slow blooming of redemption.

I understand the belly side
of torment, how scraping
legs, feet, jaw, bring relief,

just as understanding
trades death
in my uneasy truce.

Crossings

folding wakes, their colors
on the roughened surface combed
like the patterns of Italian book paper,
lustrous and promising.
    Mark Doty, "Night Ferry"

The cresting waters
of imagination
create space.

The words that sometimes
do not follow
the path my thoughts

weave through,
merge on a playground
bright with possibilities.

Consciousness swings wildly
higher and higher,
thrown into air.

Meanings land sure-footed,

run across fields, walk on pavement
through streets to find home –

beside you, yours, ours, theirs.

They incubate and foster
clarity like a sunbeam.

Yet I dig for more
than this vague dark presence

that waits for me under ivy,
covered phrases,

meant for
silvery recollection.

Play out my time.

I wonder if interpretation
breeds misunderstanding,
as a smile meant for someone else
would catch you off-guard.

What was developing
in an open-air dialogue
Is now disputed rhetoric,
the very foundation
of my being invisible.

I breaststroke through
this liquid slick of conversation,
backfloat to see the domed words.

Somewhere between the idioms
and rain there lies a truth.

I can no longer think,
only feel, listen, watch.

The point of it all sizzles
just on the tip of my tongue.

Rock the Cradle

My world does not have to be so big tomorrow
Or the next year
    William Nichols, "Turn Of Season"

I remember the deep blackness
of the crow babies,
nested high in the horse chestnut
by the side yard.

Their hungry cries
stir morning into
an early wakening.

And the mother,
who I have fed for the last year,
dive bombs me when I step off
my back porch,

not wanting to risk her babies
for a scrap of dinner,
leftovers
from my own children's mouths.

I remember being that protective once.
The kids would howl
and I ran like Billy-o

to smooth out the wrinkles
of their troubled day.

Tears and mumbled tales
of deceit were their ammunition
against duplicitous friends.

I taught them to be fierce
so the words didn't always
drop like darts
onto their bruised hearts.

The babies have begun
to squawk in hunger now.

I want to stuff
their tiny faces
until they are full

of bravado that whips
their burgeoning
wings into flight.

I'll whisper my prayer
of safe passage

and follow you
into the deepening sky

where flight is only
another lifetime away.

With the Rain

Whatever it is you are struggling
to remember
It is not poised on the tip of your tongue
    Billy Collins, "Forgetfulness"

I have seen whole nights disappear
when even Gretel can't help me
find my way back.

The forest top
is so thick, the stars
of a midnight sky
can't shake
my memory into being.

I pilfer whole strands
of the alphabet,
shuffle syllables around
the base of my tongue,
just so I can carry
you with me,
my shrunken life.

I struggle to shift
even a snapshot
of recollection.

Will I forget
the orchids
or the way you stroked
my back as I swam
the river
under a burning sun?

The sweet smell
of wild strawberries
and the thick glaze
of wet summer roads,

leads me back home,
to a simpler time –
when there was only
the moment and the day,

that I soon forgot
in the rain.

My father and me

He came out of the snow
Bones over his eyes
So he wouldn't go blind
    Lorna Crozier, "Man from the North"

My father seemed a tall man
to my children.

His white hair a signature
they kept in their pockets,

when life was too overwhelming
and they needed a memory of kindness.

For me he was a wild man,

came from the forest strong
like the trees and wild boar.

He shielded my eyes
from the look of disapproval
from strangers.

The umbrella he gripped
protected us from family squalls.

Father was a blind wolf,
coins of gold pressed
against his lids.

I followed him everywhere,
tripping on roots,

grasping at the dirt
to find my footing
in a dark wood.

He never faltered
despite endings when
mean words softened
his quiet strength.

We'd press our cheeks
against his bowed legs.

Chattered our confusion
of blindness and clarity
into the curve of his arms.

Today when I look
into my children's eyes,

I can feel his pride
and know we have done well –

my father and I.

Landlocked

This land like a mirror turns you inward
And you become a forest in a furtive lake;
  Gwendolyn MacEwen, "Dark Pines Under Water"

Walk lightly,
the swans' eyes are closed.

She is floating
like dandelion fluff
in a hard-backed lake.

Her slim-necked whiteness
swallows the rustle of reeds.

Her ghostly reflection trembles
in the sudden sweep
of the pine-scented breeze.

No one ever hears her call.

It is buried between
the silence of the purple
blaze of fireweed
and old man's beard.

It festoons the branches
like jade webs.

She pierces my gaze
with her blank-eyed glance.

Unfurls her mighty
albatross wings,

gathers water lilies
to her like magnets,
they cling to her breast as she passes.

Majestic, her story unravels
in the quiet sun.

The babies that follow
try to keep up.

She stalls, waits, moves on.
Stalls, waits, moves on.
A circular dance toward shore
keeps them in unison.

A flowing family
whispering the secrets

of the wind back at itself.

The Authors

Jude Neale is a Canadian poet, vocalist, spoken word performer and mentor. She publishes frequently in journals, anthologies, and e-zines. She was shortlisted, highly commended and finalist for many international competitions including: The Gregory O'Donoghue International Poetry Prize (Ireland), The International Poetic Republic Poetry Prize (U.K),The Mary Chalmers Smith Poetry Prize (UK), The Wenlock International Poetry Competition (UK) and the Carers International Poetry Prize (UK).

Jude has written six books.

Her book, *A Quiet Coming of Light, A Poetic Memoir* (leaf press), was a finalist for the 2015 Pat Lowther Memorial Award, five of its poems were shortlisted for The Magpie Award, judged by George McWhirter, Vancouver's first Poet Laureate, and three of its poems were nominated for the coveted Pushcart Prize (US) by three different publishers.

One of Jude's poems from her recent book, *Splendid in its Silence*, was chosen by Britain's Poet Laureate to ride with other winners around the Channel Islands on public transit for a year. Jude was a featured reader at the Guernsey International Literary festival.

This book was recently a SPM Prize winner and was published in the UK in April.

Some of these poems can be heard on Jude's collaborative (viola/spoken word) EP, *Places Beyond*.

Jude's forthcoming book, *A Blooming*, will be published in London the summer of 2018.

Bonnie Nish is Executive Director of Pandora's Collective Outreach Society. Bonnie has been widely published worldwide in such places as *The Ottawa Arts Review*, *The Danforth Review*, *Haunted Waters Press*, *Illness Crisis & Loss Journal Volume 24* and *The Blue Print Review*.

She has won prizes for her writing and work has been performed to both music and dance all over North America including at the Palace of the Legion of Honours in San Francisco.

Bonnie's first book of poetry *Love and Bones* was released by Karma Press in 2013.

Bonnie has a Masters in Arts Education from Simon Fraser University and is currently pursuing a PhD in Language and Literacy Education at UBC.

Her latest book *Concussion and Mild TBI: Not Just Another Headline*, an anthology of concussion-related stories, was published by Lash and Associates in August 2016.

Bonnie has conducted writing and expressive arts workshops for over 20 years across North America.